ISBN 978-0-259-49625-0
PIBN 10105667

1 MONTH OF
FREE
READING

at

www.ForgottenBooks.com

By purchasing this book you are eligible for one month membership to ForgottenBooks.com, giving you unlimited access to our entire collection of over 1,000,000 titles via our web site and mobile apps.

To claim your free month visit:

www.forgottenbooks.com/free105667

145

THE
EASTERN QUESTION;

— A —

SUMMARY VIEW OF IT

—FOR—

BUSY MEN,

—BY—

ONE OF THEMSELVES.

HARRISBURG, PA:
1876.

ERRATA.

Page 16, *eighteenth line from top for* philanthropy *read* philosophy.
Page 20, *nineteenth line from top for* sea *read* seat.

THE

EASTERN QUESTION;

— A —

SUMMARY VIEW OF IT

— FOR —

BUSY MEN,

— BY —

ONE OF THEMSELVES.

———————

HARRISBURG, PA:
CHAS. H. BERGNER.
1876.

TO THE HON. SIMON CAMERON,

OF PENNSYLVANIA,

CHAIRMAN OF THE COMMITTEE ON FOREIGN RELATIONS

IN THE

SENATE OF THE UNITED STATES.

An uninterrupted friendship of more than thirty years has induced the writer to address the few pages following to you. And further, it seemed appropriate so to do, seeing that no servant of the people is likely to have the subject more frequently brought before him than yourself in your official capacity as Chairman of the most important Committee to whom it may be referred. Should this production be considered in that committee by yourself and your colleagues as simply a fair "case stated," that will be as high an honor as its writer could hope for it.

HARRISBURG, PENN'A, November, 1876.

ADVERTISEMENT.

The writer of the ensuing pages has seen, as the whole world has seen for some time past, The Eastern Question looming above the horizon of cotemporary history, and becoming more and more portentous day by day.

As it grew into prominence he naturally asked himself what it really meant, and not being able fully to answer, he sought an explanation of it in the organs of public opinion and instruction, the periodical press.

Still disappointed of a satisfactory solution, and believing that there were many others like himself, he looked for information from other sources within his reach, and has found the following, which he gives to the public for what it is worth.

This little pamphlet is intended for the active, industrious men of business and daily occupation, who have not time to investigate multitudinous sources of information; and hence, also, the prominent and important facts are in some cases repeated, that the gist of the case may be impressed upon the memory of the reader. Nor is an apology offered for such iteration, as it was intentional with the object stated.

Should the effect of this publication be but to draw from some superior source a better explication of the subject, the writer will be fully rewarded for his trouble.

THE EASTERN QUESTION.

Those are three simple words—but they contain an amount of meaning in the present and coming history of this world which might require volumes to settle in language—and may probably require lakes of blood to be shed before a solution leaving the world in peace can be attained.

A singular fact exists in the order of Providence—and it is this—the Eastern Hemisphere having been first settled by mankind, contains the most numerous populations—and portions of that hemisphere, the Eastern portions, have become, and indeed since history began, have always proved themselves to be the most densely populated.

China and Hindostan number to the square mile 'a figure in population such that we can scarcely conceive how it is possible such numbers can be sustained. Imagine from four hundred and fifty to five hundred to the square mile, and compare it to our ten or fifteen. Competition reduces wages—and the rate of wages is inversely in proportion with the population. The more numerous the population, the lower the rate. In China and the East Indies, then including the Islands, we find wages always extremely low—a rate of about one-twentieth or so, only five cents in the dollar to the rate in western Europe —and this fact has existed from a period in which the memory of man goeth not to the contrary. It was so in the Babylonian times—in the Grecian times—in the times of the Carthagenians and the Romans—and it is so to-day. Now the inhabitants of the East Indies, both of the mainland and of the Archipelagoes, have always been extremely industrious—and let what will be said, they have always been and are ingenious and useful mechanics. They have always produced fabrics, both useful and ornamental, which created a market amongst the Western nations. The Western nations have always desired to possess and use these products and fabrics, and were always willing to pay a fair price for them. But what is a fair price? It is what they would be worth if produced amongst themselves where wages are twenty times higher than they were in the producing countries.

This fact has always then excited the cupidity of the merchandising and trading nations and individuals. The element of the cost of a thing in the East Indies is the result of the rate of wages there—and a thing can be bought in those countries, therefore, for five cents—which in the Western nations is not considered dear at a dollar.

Add the cost of transportation to the cost of the article in the East Indies, and that is the cost of it in the Atlantic nations.

Here, then, is the inducement which creates a commercial nation. In ancient times the nations in nearest proximity with the East grew in consequence of a monopoly of this trade. Hence your Babylons and your Syrias, the dense and powerful and wealthy associations of men in the rich provinces to the East of the Mediterranean. Then sprung up, probably the outcropping of those countries—selected communities settling upon the Islands of the Mediterranean and its maritime coasts—the Greeks, the Sicilians, the Carthagenians, the Romans. Some of these became producing communities—others trading or commercial nations, who bought in the cheapest markets and sold in the dearest. Carthage was always a trading nation—a nation of sailors and trafficking adventurers—who, understanding navigation, attained maritime predominance. She purchased of the Grecians, and supplied their wants. But Greece having risen to prominence amongst the nations of the Mediterranean again sank into obscurity, not having been sustained by a reasonable system of religion, without which no nation can permanently exist. Then sprung up the Romans, and Rome became a depot for its back country, the Peninsula of Italy. Its beginning was founded in the purest morality and virtue attainable probably by mankind. Unfortunately in casting her anchor in heaven, (to make use of a beautiful figure of some French author, for the establishment of a national religion,) she did not choose such an anchor as would hold there. She might have made a much better choice than she did. Whilst Remus and Romulus were being suckled by the wolf, Isaiah was preaching in the Holy Land. Ah ! if she could but have heard him, and listened to the truths of the Single Godhead. Had she adopted the Hebraic belief, short of absolute perfection as it was, but closely approaching it. Had she listened to the Hebraic teaching instead of the Hellenic, how different might have been the result.

Had the sublime and holy doctrines of Isaiah been taken in by the early Romans, instead of the ingenious, comprehensive, poetical, nay beautiful and attractive, but fantastic system of the Grecian mythology, how different might have been the result to mankind? But glare and glitter, poetry and sentiment, artistic but human philosophy, indebted not in the least to divine revelation, but evolved alone from the poetical imaginations of intellectual men; these were the foundations of the system of morality chosen for their guidance by the bold, daring, heroic, virtuous, practical Romans. The religion they chose was of the earth earthy, so ingeniously arranged as to seem to cover the whole ground, but possessing not one single scintillation of the heavenly ray. The Hebraic revelations—the older Testament—if known, were set aside. The homely morality of the agricultural Hebrews was not attractive to this otherwise great people,—the poetical myths in infinite variety, the result of the philosophical reflections of the most intelligent and imaginative people that the world has seen before or since. The artistic arrangement of the Grecian mythological system proved more attractive to the heroic Romans, and they were carried away by it, in an evil hour. It is impossible to estimate what this cost them. Had they listened to Isaiah, how much stronger would their celestial hold have been?—nay, they had no celestial hold. Isaiah would have given them the Mosaic system—they might have become children of Israel, and the coming of Christ might long have been delayed. But it was in the hands of the Almighty, and He suffered the Romans to choose as they did—perhaps to teach those who came after them, how small the dependence which is to be placed in a merely hu_ man system of ethics.

We see now the result of the first forty centuries of the world's history in this favorite seat of mankind. Let us examine this chosen area. If a point be taken in the Mediterranean sea, and an ellipse be constructed about that point at the intersection of the two diameters, such that the semi-con_ gugate diameter shall be from a thousand to fifteen hundred miles, and the semi-transverse be from fifteen hundred to two thousand miles in length; that area—the area of that ellipse—will about include the birth-place of the most important races of mankind which have yet existed on our planet; not the most numerous, but the strongest and most intelligent; all the great events of history preceding the Advent, occurred within this area. The greatest poets, painters, sculptors, heroes, philosophers, historians, warriors, prophets, navigators, travelers—even our Lord himself—first appeared within this area. The garden of Eden was within it, and to-day are to be found there climates and scenery approaching our idea of the Elysian in character.

Nay, within this area are now to be seen the finest physical specimens of men and women on the earth, the nearest approach both to masculine and feminine beauty. And why should it not be so? The very air that is breathed there is the most salubrious on the world's surface. This area then was the seat of the grandest of the race, and it was sustained by the acci- dents of its physical geography. Here existed the Mediterranean sea, properly so called, for was it not the middle of the earth at that time.

This ocean was surrounded by land on all sides. Its limits were known. It penetrated the superficies of the hemisphere for a distance of some three thousand miles. There were none of its coasts that were not fertile—none of its islands unproductive.

Man extended himself about it. He settled on the islands. He moved back from the coasts. He cultivated the soil and supported himself. He came back to the ports for his luxuries, his amusements, or to enjoy his wealth. He in some cases, wandered so far off that he became isolated from his fellows, and reverted to barbarism. But this was the home, this was the seat of em- pire. Here were the Babylons, the Ninevehs, the Bagdads, the Alexandrias, the Romes, the Cairos.

Here he passed over four thousand years. We have slight glimpses of what he did in the unsatisfactory scraps of history and poetry which have come down to us. But these are so mixed with personal adventures, ambi- tions, conflicts, aims and failures of individuals, that one can take no inter- est in them. The history of an ambitious man in one age is a mere rescript of that in another. Say, for instance, how nearly alike, in some generic re- spects, are Cæsar and Napoleon. By the way, both of them originating within one hundred miles of each other in this Mediterranean country, and ravaging the world until they had occasioned the slaughter of millions of their fellow men, leaving no appreciable result, unless the thinning out of the race had been proposed at their birth. In looking at history it is what races did that we want to know. How came they to increase and multiply here, and to attenuate and fall away there? Those are the questions. Mankind in creased in our Mediterranean ellipsis because it was easy for him to live on the products of the land and the waters, and when the competition for exist- ence became too great he would emigrate back from the shores. Some na- tions would cultivate navigation and commercial adventure, attaining in one place cheaply what they could sell in another at profit.

The Mediterranean furnished ample room for this. What man wanted on the coasts of Spain, or on the shores of the Adriatic, these traders—ped- dlers, if you please—would go off and fetch for him from the shores of the Black sea, meeting there merchants with their caravans from the interior, who had bought at very low prices, and had the articles for sale at a fair profit. Or boats could be poled up the Euphrates from the Persian Gulf. Or the dangers of the Red Sea might be encountered, to bring up the strange things from Africa or Asia. Greece came into existence, it is impossible to imagine how, unless by spontaneous selection of the best and fittest from the other crowds of men. For how could such a language, how could such arts, how could such philosophy, such poetry, such oratory; nay, such an ingenious ar- rangement of a religion and code of morality originate amongst any promis- cuous average assemblage of men.

Athens was scarcely bigger than the present area of the city of Philadel- phia. It flourished, as it is called, only for about three hundred years, and see what was done in that period of time by that handful of people. What architecture, sculpture, poetry, oratory—models in all for all future times, never to be surpassed—which, now that we are familiar with them for thou- sands of years, we are always endeavoring to emulate, yet never reaching.

Greece came and asserted intellectual superiority. Content with that. Other communities sought wealth, and others, working for their neighbors, trafficked. Carthage and Sicily probably excelled in this until Rome came and dominated them all.

Rome made its city its rendezvous for the best and strongest. It set up a republic, and lived a severely proper and just life. It strengthened from all sides—from behind and in front. It commanded the respect of its fellows. The Greeks became effeminate, and Rome took the lead. It must have been, too, a great trading city—must have monopolized the markets. Carthage, as has been said, set up for this, and Carthage undertook to drive Rome out of competition—tried it for nearly three centuries. But the force- ful Romans at last gathering their whole strength struck a final blow, and *Delenda est Carthago.*

Rome grew and grew, riped and riped, and alas, rotted and rotted, and thereby hangs a tale. But all this time man had free chance to go where he pleased to buy things to sell again. To be sure there were pirates, things and men *in transitu*, were in the old times levied on as they are to-day. But the pirates were fought and kept down. Man could trade, subject only to the levies legal or other made upon his things. He submitted to the pirate, occasionally fighting, as he submits now to the railroad kings whose legalized impositions perhaps exceed in proportion the piracies, robberies and tributes of the old days.

So far as mere morality is concerned, Rome was perhaps as permanently founded as any simply human society can be founded. The rights of man were acknowledged; but classes, unfortunately, were recognized. There is so much difference between the best and the worst, the highest and the lowest of men, that the arrangement of equal laws for all has invariably proved a stumbling block against the advancement of any human society.

Rome wanted to do right, and so long as the higher classes behaved with absolute impartiality, she advanced and succeeded. But she grew in numbers, and numbers begat competition, and jealousy, and ambition. The anchor in heaven, if it had any hold at all, had not a very strong hold. The religion of the Romans was not spiritual. Their gods were human. They had human passions. The fables respecting them, are stories, such as may be told of men; indeed, similar traces may be found in all religions, until after the Advent. But the Grecian mythology gave the history of men, great men to be sure, possessing higher powers than man—up to infinite strength and grandeur; but they were men, and the goddesses were women.

How, then, could any human community, under the auspices of a set of imaginary great *men*, act otherwise than as men? The vices of mankind surround all societies, with a certain pressure, and they will leak in through the most impervious human covering.

The purity of the Roman republic lasted, then, but a short time; a few generations. Factions, instigated by jealousy, sprung up, and soon after, civil war. The Roman republic may be said to have prospered as a model society, or commonwealth, for perhaps three hundred years, and then commenced civil wars. which became chronic, continuing for four hundred years longer; the Republic preserving itself in a fashion, living on its traditions, until at last it ended, and the Empire took its place, on the death—by assassination—of Julius Cæsar. Then came greatness, magnificence, conquest, wealth, luxury, corruption, and, at last, death. If it be not impious to conceive motives for the Almighty—to describe Him as a personage in history—one would say that He saw and knew what the end would be, and almost simultaneously with the commencement of the Roman empire He sent his Son into the world, so that his teachings would take root and strengthen the newly planted social arrangement. Cæsar had not been dead fifty years until Christ was born. Men fondly thought that the Cæsarean plant was to thrive, but it was a far different plant which was to thrive.

The empire of this world was not to be held by a Cæsar, nor under a political system promulgated by a Cæsar. No, the system was to originate with the poorest and humblest of men. A baby was born in a manger, who was to grow up and, reaching man's estate, was to preach to a few fishermen and peasants a doctrine which, truly followed, would lead to both earthly and heavenly happiness—which, neglected or falsely administered, would bring ruin and atrophy, like the others, upon those who thus mistook it.

Rome listened not at first to the lowly preacher and the fishermen. Rome, on the contrary, persecuted Him and His followers. Him she permitted to be crucified; them she maltreated and worried for three hundred years, the while she herself was rotting and rotting. But the plant took root—the grain of mustard seed germinated, increased and multiplied slowly, like a vegetable, growing, spreading, but making no noise. Rome commenced its empire about the time that the Son of Man commenced His—Rome, the mistress of the world; Christ, the leader of a few fishermen and peasants.

The one burnt the candle at both ends, conquered and swelled, and rioted—and fell; and great was the fall thereof. Men were left perfectly exhausted, all their energies gone, except the muscular energy of the savage. The other was left to revivify the mass.

But meantime the land was there—the Mediterranean was there and its surroundings; men still remained upon the ground; savages, if you like; but still men—men of the old races. But there was no government. All kinds of government had been tried and failed. The followers of the Son of Man were there, but they dared not assume government. They believed in their Christ; they lived peaceable, unassuming lives; they tried to imitate Him. For three hundred years, while Rome was burning herself out—dying of cancer—they stood martyrdom and persecution. They were like their Master, despised and rejected of men; but they lived on. They worshiped in caves; they preserved the Testament of the Lord. They came and went, sought no honors, watched and prayed, and when the Master called them, they were ready. The thoughtless at last even began to observe them. Persecuted though these people were, they were happy even here. They quarreled not amongst themselves; they worshiped the Master and bided their time. Unknown almost to themselves, they increased; the doctrines spread imperceptibly. Their preachers were the very best men in the world, and their influence increased, until in, say five hundred years, bad, ambitious men became attached to them, perceiving that they might be made a power in the land. The idea of an earthly body, called the Church, became a fixed fact. To be at the head of this Church, was to possess immense power. This headship, however, could not be obtained as empire could be obtained. The members of the Church must be men of decent, orderly lives. Splendor and magnificence were not at first elements or accompaniments of power in the Church; men must be at least outwardly good to obtain this power, and, accordingly, the first possessors of it were at least outwardly good and orderly. The Headship of the Church was at last established. Authority was sought for it and found. The remark of Jesus to Peter was taken as sufficient authority upon which to build a society which should rule mankind, and the head of this society should be, ex-officio, the supreme governor of the world.

For the first few years, nay it may be said for a century or two, this system, continuously administered, served to reknit society together. Fairly virtuous, good men attained the headship of the Christian society, and men gradually settled down to peaceable occupations. They cultivated the soil, they turned their hands to manufactures, they were not nine-tenths of them soldiers, ravaging the fields of the peaceful husbandmen. Rome's grandeur decayed. Rome had been overrun by savages. She no longer sent goverors to her distant provinces. The provinces reverted to anarchy, and by degrees the feudal system sprung up.

Thus Britain, Germany, France, Spain—all North and West of the Mediterranean commenced *de novo*, reverting first from the colonial system of Rome to absolute anarchy and gradually coming to life again through the feudal system, until government settled itself in the form of monarchy. All these were aided by the spread of Christianity. Rome from being the political governess of the world became the High Priestess of the world, and was in all cases the *imperium in imperio*. The more Southern nations were slower to rise out of heathenism, and amongst them Christianity did not take root. All this was natural. Christianity was too pure for the warm-blooded Southrons. A more sensuous, a more sensual system they would naturally take in, and although Christ himself arose amongst them; the masses did not take to Him as their more northern fellow creatures did. The northern nations had passed through hundreds of years of civil war and bloodshed. To violence had followed exhaustion. They sought rest and peace, and Christianity inculcated peace. For were they not enjoined when stricken on the right cheek to turn the left for a second stroke.

There was then in the South anarchy in politics, and anarchy in religion, until, in the seventh century, Mahomet arose, and because Mahomet represented a sensual heaven, the heaven he represented was accepted by them. The southern nations were not yet worn out so much by war, and they thirsted for conquest.

This was the state of things when he flourished, and large portions of northern Africa and southeastern Asia flocked to his standard—the crescent. The Ottoman empire flourished and spread over vast areas of the earth, aiming eventually to conquer with the sword the whole world.

It must be remembered that the whole world was then supposed to be embraced in our ellipsis.

For was not the Mediterranean the only navigable sea, save the Atlantic coasts. The main ocean, illimitable to the westward, as it was believed to be, was never attempted. The whole world was northern Africa and its accessories, southern and southeastern Europe and its accessories, and southwestern Asia and its accessories.

This was the state of things. Christianity was spreading, and, to a certain extent, enlightening mankind on the upper coasts of the Mediterranean and the back countries: in Spain, France, Italy, Austria, Hungary, Germany, Russia. On the lower coasts of the Mediterranean, the Ottoman power was gaining and conquering and extending.

The influence of Rome over her old colonies was strong, but as yet it was purely spiritual. Politically those nations were being born again. Mankind on the whole, might be called at rest. He was recuperating. The same blood, mixed to an extent by the political mutations of Rome, occupied the same areas. He still possessed the old capabilities. But he was tired and needed rest. But he must live, he must trade, he must produce, he must exchange products, and societies of men feeling themselves fitted for these occupations would engage in them. Sailors and merchants were one and the same in the old times. The great merchant was probably first an adventurous skipper. He would build or purchase a vessel and he would start out on a venture. He would take the products of his own region, scour around the coasts of the Mediterranean, sell his cargo, purchase another, and return to his port of embarkation.

At the period we are now contemplating some enterprising merchants shrewdly chose the head of the Adriatic as a depot of trade—a most admirable choice it was, too. For look at its accessibility from the interior and its immense back country. Look at its accessibility by water. The Adriatic trends due North and South for hundreds of miles. Its coasts are rich in products. The Eastern bases of the Appenines and their rich valleys are tributary to it. The left bank is more productive still, and it leads southward for the Asian and African trade. Communicating with the Mediterranean it communicated with all the coasts. The Red Sea could be reached, using a short portage ; so could the Persian Gulf, in the same way. And with the aid of the Euphrates the East Indian products could be got. Our skipper could purchase things East that cost in labor at the rate of five cents a day, and could take them home and sell them where labor cost one dollar per day, not perhaps in these exact figures but in this proportion, clearing the difference, minus only the cost of transportation. Surely this was a good trade, and no wonder then that our skippers who set up their little depot at the head of the Adriatic prospered in their business.

They were enterprising men, these Venetians. See what they did. There was no good port at the head of the Adriatic—the shores were marshy and shoal; but they found a bar, with a good foundation to it, in sufficiently deep water some distance out from the shore. Here they built their wharves and warehouses, founding them upon the rock probably, or on piles, and between their warehouses their vessels could float and be unloaded. The main shore was communicated with by bridges and causeways, and what came from the land, reached the warehouses by that means.

There must have been first-rate engineers in the employ of those merchant traders and skippers, for they have left wonderful works behind them. Indeed, the Romans had great engineers amongst them. See their aqueducts, sewers; sea walls, &c., some of them standing uninjured to this day. The Venetians appreciated the Adriatic, for did she not bring them all their wealth? Caravans from the Caspian, and from the frosty Caucasus would ship on the Black Sea, and then through the Bosphorus and the Dardanelles the ships would work north, up the Adriatic. The Venetians appreciated that arm of the Mediterranean, for was not there performed a marriage ceremony yearly, whereby the Adriatic was "wedded to our Duke?" Had the Adriatic divorced herself and left Venice high and dry, it would have been a pity, and bad for Venice; but she never did. Yearly she brought the treasures of the world to the great mart, and the merchants of Venice became princes. But this was not to last forever. It lasted more than half a millenium, and during that time the city reached the highest stage of municipal grandeur. Such architecture—such engineering—such cathedrals—such palaces! Has not Ruskin written a whole book on the mere "Stones of Venice?" But time eats things. The same circumstances were not always to continue. The sailors on the Atlantic coast were not idle all this time; the Portuguese especially became extremely ventursome. Lisbon was a great port for the outside world, and there the hardy sailors used to ship for all parts. At last one more daring than the rest, kept sailing and sailing south and south, but following the coast. It trended east, and still following, it trended north again; and all at once our Portuguese skipper found himself round the corner, calling the corner the Cape of Good Hope. The new sea was penetrated, and the East Indies was reached by water. This put a new face on the commerce of the world. For some years the Lisbon merchants monopolized the trade. The English wanted it, but as yet they dare not venture on the voyage over an unknown ocean. Their merchants at first contented themselves with turning pirates and buccaneers, attacking the unwieldy Portuguese carracks, as they were called. At first they would appropriate the cargoes and destroy the vessels; but at last they got to dismantling the great massive hulks, and towing them bodily into the port of London. Soon, however, the jolly jack tars of Britain ventured around the Cape themselves, and once familiarized to the new ocean, their bold adventurous character took the lead there, elbowing all others away. England determined upon monopolizing the trade, and the shortest way to do that was to monopolize the country. The Dutch had followed the Portuguese into the Indian Ocean somewhat prior to the English, and when the English began the business, they had both the Dutch and the Portuguese to get rid of. They fought the Dutch out of all their possessions there, except Java, which they have left to them to this day. The Portuguese, England enticed into a sort of partnership, which still exists, and is based upon the equitable principle of "heads I win, tails you lose." She protects(?) Portugal in the enjoyment of her rights, as against all claiming or to claim upon her; and Portugal was lulled to sleep quietly, whilst the great East India company came into existence—a corporation governing politically some two hundred millions of people. These latter events occurred between about 1480 and 1600—the discovery of the Cape and the establishment of the East India company. To-day Great Britain enjoys the monopoly of the great East India trade, and holds empire over the two hundred millions of people and their territory, at a distance equal to the semi-circumference of the earth from the seat of the sovereign.

America was discovered about the same time, and that gave additional activity to the business of the sea. England interested herself in the Northern hemisphere, and Spain in the Southern. Not, however, without strong and bloody opposition from the English. But this did not disturb the monopoly of the East India trade, which England "went in to see." It was a big thing. Workmen to the number of some four or five hundred millions, including those of the Chinese empire, constantly at work, producing useful things. Things for which there was always a demand, producing them at the rate of four or five cents per day for their wages, whilst at the markets where they were sold the wages were more than ten times as high. Six days' worth of cotton in India would cost, say twenty-five or thirty cents in money. Six days' worth of cotton in England would cost three or four dollars. The freight would have to be added to the cost in India. That would not be more than four or five cents more. Then the profit would be the difference between thirty or thirty-five cents and three or four dollars. Good trade, of course, it was, and England kept an eye almost single upon it. Her grasp of it never relaxed—relaxes not at this moment. This Good Hope way turned out to be much cheaper, and certainly much safer than any way possible to the Venetians, and do what she could Venice could not retain the trade. For just about the same time another thing happened, or at least .was fully consummated. This was the Empire of the Turk over the countries through which the Venetian avenues of trade existed. Constantinople had been taken in the middle of the fifteenth century. Mahomet II., who took it, died about 1480, and from the moment the Turk got possession an era of proscription commenced. There was no such thing known as free egress and regress.

The region taken by the Turk was rich beyond compare. It could sustain him and his wives, and what more did he care for? He left the rest to destiny. As for regularity of trade in the Mediterranean, of that there was none. Italy had slept for a thousand years—more than a thousand years under church government. The Vatican and its twenty-five thousand priests in Rome, must be sustained undisturbed. The Turk could loll upon his couches at Constantinople amongst his three hundred wives. Sporting with Amayllis in the shade, or with the tangles of Nerea's hair. Poor Venice lost her trade, and no longer could her doges court the Adriatic by throwing a valuable ring into her bosom annually. The Spaniard showed some of his old Iberian energy. Columbus under his auspices had discovered America, South America. The Spaniard developed the wealth of Peru—the gold and the precious stones of the Andes. He became rich in the precious metals. England disputed his every step, though ineffectually. But the twenty-five thousand priests at the Vatican, and other ecclesiastical obligations, hung upon him. The Spaniard possessed the fatal gift of believing those whom he trusted; he became of "the Faithful"—the faithful par excellence—those who believed in Mother Church. The Pope was the vicegerent of God—was infallible. The Spaniard believed in him then—believes in him now. And what is the net result? Why he retains a single island out of half a hemisphere which was once his. What though the new world was peopled with Spaniards, as noble a race naturally as is to be found anywhere, but credulous to a fault. The priests have hung upon him for century after century, until at last he is scarcely himself. But the aggressive Englishman pinned his faith to no man's sleeve. He thought for himself. If his monarch ordered him to believe in a certain way against his judgment he would either desert his monarch and go somewhere else to pray, or he would cut off his monarch's head and teach him and his descendants that he would not be trifled with. The Englishman would have his free bible and read it for himself. He thought he could work out his own salvation. He would have priests, to be sure, for teachers, but the priests must keep within bounds. John Bull will not be humbugged, to use his own phrase, by anybody. The Church tried it, but the Englishman kicked against the pricks and made a Pope at home to suit himself. Nor would the Englishman stand too much political nonsense either. He colonized North America, and when the folks at home interfered too much, he set up for himself in a large part of the territory, and in respect to those parts, where he continued the connection, the folk at home have to "behave," or they would be lost. But, to go back to our Mediterranean country.

As an area through which free transportation of men and things could be effected, the whole region—land and water—fell into comparative desuetude. The Turk guarded the straits between the Black sea and the Mediterranean; he swayed the banks of the Euphrates. Egypt ruled over the Isthmus of Suez, and had not risen out of heathanism, or had become Mussulman. The English got possession of points in the Mediterranean, and finally of the Straits of Gibralter. The Czar often aimed at driving the Turk out of Europe, but, somehow, was never able to do so. The Czar had at one time a certain trade at Sebastopol, but—it was not worth while keeping it up. France, fronting on the Mediterranean, while Napoleon was strutting among the nations like a bantam cock, conceived through him the idea of conquering Egypt, and making the Mediterranean a "French lake." It was a saying of his that the empire of the world should have its seat at Constantinople. But the English soon put an end to the haughty little despot, much as he had fluttered, and crowed, and clucked about Europe for a score or so of years. Austria—always bigoted—gave too much of her time to his Holiness. And Italy was absolutely ruled by the Fisherman.

In short, this part of the world—all of it—through ignorance, superstition, diversity of language, and weakness, the remains of old disturbances—this part of the world, the very garden bed of mankind, where the greatest and best of the whole race have all originated; where the most beautiful specimens exist now—a region capable of being the centre of the seat of empire for the whole earth—by location, climate, physical geography, richness of soil, and every possible material advantage—this region is now sparsely populated by a large variety of the race whose energies, once the most powerful on the earth, have weakened and become flaccid, enervated, useless.

Is this to continue? *That is part of the Eastern question.*

The causes of emulation and competition between the peoples exist at this moment, as they existed in the times of the Punic wars, over two thousand years ago. Here is the region that was the civilized world for nearly four thousand years. We see now what mankind can do in a century. Certainly he must have been doing something during the first forty centuries of history in this geographical area, included in this ellipse of, say thirty-five hundred by twenty-five hundred miles. Here was a fine ocean, irregular in form, protruding north, protruding south, in the temperate, and a small part in the torrid zone—extending further east and west than north and south—uniting the atlantic coast with the frontiers of the dense eastern populations, where wages were from three to five cents a day for fourteen to eighteen hours hard work. The product of this labor for sale—nations competing to buy—this competition producing wars, disruption, piracies, buckaneering, freebooting, called fillibustering by the half-breeds of Central America. Rome destroyed Carthage. She herself was sunk by the Goths and Vandals. Venice sprung up and, as a free city, enjoyed this business snugly for herself—favored so by the Adriatic that her Doge would be married to her every year.

The Head of the Church was in Rome. He found that these peoples were easy of belief—eminently "faithful," and the temptation was too much for frail man, for the vicegerent of God, after all, was but a man.   *philosophy*

Italy excelled not only in the arts, in poetry, in ~~philanthropy~~, in politics, but in *belief*, as did all the nations surrounding the Mediterranean. Belief—a capacity for believing, was their prominent feature. It became the Church's stock in trade. Did she not name them the Faithful, par excellence. With this she influenced them all as she wished. The Church was the most magnificent close corporation that ever existed in the world. She ruled them all. But the first interests to be attended to were her temporal interests. They might advance, they might become enlightened, they might have arts, poetry, eloquence, but true philosophy, *not*. That might interfere with belief, and belief was her stock in trade, as we say. Were they not all the Faithful and was she not God's representative here on earth, deriving her powers immediately from God's hand? There must be no investigating the creation. The Church knew as much of that as was necessary. The earth cannot go round the sun, said the Church, and if you say it can you shall go to prison. What business have you with this? If God thinks it proper that I should be enlightened on this subject He will enlighten me. I am His representative. So the Church would have its finger in all temporalities. Republics sprung up in Italy. The profoundest thinkers on human polity framed them, tried to sustain them. The constitutions were based on the rights of man, but unless supervised by the Church they were of Satan—not of God—and so the republics could not last. After the Goths subjugated Rome apathy came—anarchy—then every man for himself. The feudal system—the simple plan sufficed for them, that they should take who had the power, and they should keep who could do so by force or strength.

The Church, however, notwithstanding all this, divided within itself. If there could be a Pope at Rome why not then a Patriarch at Constantinople. There was room for two—and two accordingly set up to rule, and so rule to this day. But Mahomet put in his oar. He came some centuries later, and sat down near the Bosphorus. If two spiritual chiefs, why not three? And three it is. The Patriarch and the Prophet's representative at Byzantium, St. Peter's at Rome, all these find their account in the credulity of mankind, and none of them cares to have him enlightened. If left to his free will he might not be so liberal to the Church; so he must be allowed to remain in a certain state of ignorance, nor be permitted to rouse himself from it. But the outsiders; the British from the $U_{lti}m_a$ Thule became adventurous sailors; not so bright as those of the more Southern coasts, but bold, dashing fellows in sight of land. The Lusitanians got round the Cape, and the British not having vessels for such navigation, or, perhaps, sailors who would dare such unknown waters, had small quick sailing shallops, or cutters, or clippers, and these would attack the heavy East India men and relieve them of their cargoes, or tow them bodily into their ports. Until from that beginning they built "tall amirals" for themselves, who could sail beyond the Cape of Good Hope, and after pass Mozambic, where far to sea northeast winds blow Sabean odors from the spicy shores of Araby the Blest.

Poor Venice lost her trade, and our garden spot was left unnoticed. Under cultivation, to be sure, but with three gardeners—the Pontiff of Rome, and the Patriarch and the Prophet's representative at Constantinople.

Nearly four centuries of this state of things has brought the world to its present condition of advancement. The way to the East has been the open ocean.

England soon saw that to monopolize the trade she must conquer the territory. For were there not sailors equal to hers at Amsterdam, at Lisbon? Along the coasts of Spain? Spain was rich enough. The Pope had given her South America in exchange for the exclusive tutelage of her people, and the Andes poured their wealth into her lap. She dreamed of conquering the world, but always under the guidance and by permission of his Holiness. Ah what a noble race has been atrophied here. The Cids, the Cortez, the sons of the men who had well-nigh baffled the Cæsars in the olden time. What capacities were not possessed by this splendid strain of blood. A nation for which it became a necessity that a poet should create an immortal romance, the object of which was to restrain the individuals of it from running mad on the subject of chivalry.

For what is chivalry? Is it not the highest conceivable tone of manly virtue in its every branch? Is it not the impersonation or embodiment of truth, and honor, and generosity, and courtesy, and valor? What is chivalry? Is it not the spiritual essence that creates the true gentleman? And what a race of men that must have been, for whom its brightest genius felt that it was incumbent upon him to write his master-piece for the sake of preventing its undue overgrowth. A part of chivalry is fidelity, a capacity for believing. The Pontiff had only to gain the confidence of this splendid nation; but once to attract its belief, to call its people the children of the Church itself, and after that he could guide it as he pleased. The result? Why Spain has resunk almost to the apathy that existed at the breaking up of the Roman empire.

This noble, intelligent, bright, manly, proud, chivalrous nation is to-day, in the nineteenth century, scarcely less noticed in the world than it was in the nineteenth year of the first century of Christ. This glorious nation is known more by this single production of its poet or romancer than by all the rest of its deeds. The pabulum of Rome breeds the disease called atrophy.

Spain has lost all her West Indian possessions, save a single island. Once having conquered a continent—the continent is gone and she owns but an island which exists in a chronic state of rebellion. But the Pope gave not up possession of South America when the Spanish monarchy gave it up. He feeds his spiritual food to the republics which gained their autonomies from the Spanish parent country, and it is doing its sure work there.

A faint endeavor has been made to show what the garden spot of the world was in the old time, and is in the new. Let us recapitulate, and as it were, index it in a few words. It is an ellipse about three thousand to three thousand five hundred miles East and West, and two thousand to two thousand five hundred North and South. It is pervaded by navigable inland seas in connection in all directions. It was the seat of the empires of mankind in the first three or four thousand years of the world. The history of that ancient period is dark to us. We know very little about it. But mankind, the most restless, the most active of all animals, must have been doing something in those old days. We cannot say exactly what it was. That history opens upon us with the Greeks, who knew everything almost better than we do, and had brighter talents than we have ever had. As has been said, we have never been able to reach its beauty of expression, in language, painting, sculpture or architecture, and say what we may, we have added but little to its knowledge of ethics. God sent us his Son to confirm some of its lessons, and add to them what remained to be added.

Its language, its vernacular talk is a study requiring the brightest of our geniuses to master. It left us examples of virtue that we never have surpassed. Can we show in all our annals a Socrates, a Homer, a Demosthenes, an Aristotle, a Cato, a Praxiteles, a Phidias, even an Alexander. These are what the four thousand first years left us. And they were all produced in' this garden spot. Then followed the Romans, only not so bright as the Greeks, but more practical, more powerful. They conquered the world, and if they did not surpass in kind they added in quantity to the legacies of the Greeks. Mankind then almost sank back into barbarism, and out of that barbarism he is rising. He could not surpass the old knowledge, but he has extended some of its branches. Pondering on the lessons of Euclid he has found out the mechanism of the heavens; pondering on those of Archimedes he has developed the steam engine, and he may be said, perhaps, to have also developed the printing press. This is about all he has done, but it is a very great deal. Having discovered an easier way to the East than the old ones, the seat of wealth changed and with the seat of wealth changed the seat of power. A brave little handful of islanders sat down upon another garden spot, somewhat cooler and healthier than the old one, and these little fellows waxed fat and kicked. They had no territory to speak of, but what they had was healthy, and a mixture of the best and most adventurous races of mankind settling on that island became sailors—adventurous bold sailors. Learning their trade thoroughly they became captains, and finally masters of the seas.

They monopolized the eastern trade until their city became another Rome, greater than the former, if anything. They conquered the East, not penetrating to it by land but sailing round to it on the ocean, reaching it easier than they could by land. The races of the old garden spot reverting to their original state suffered the spiritual element to enter into all their temporal institutions, and the spiritual element, or its teachers rather, ruled them through the mysteries which they pretended to know, whilst the islanders without ignoring the spiritual principle, would not be ruled by it in temporalities; acknowledged it in its place, but kept it there. This not without a serious struggle, but a struggle that ended in success. The islanders have an anchor in heaven, but they render unto God only the things that are God's; retaining for Cæsar the things that are Cæsar's.

These islanders then, as they say in their national song, "rule the waves;" their flag has braved, for a thousand years, the battle and the breeze. The races about the Mediterranean have slept, or have, perhaps, deteriorated. Yet, there is the lovely climate; there is the glorious midland ocean; there are the mountains; there are the valleys that produced the Greeks and Romans. Are there not some of the old seeds left?

It has been reported, that in unfolding some mummies which had lain in an Egyptian mausoleum for three thousand years, some dry grains of wheat were discovered which, from the unchangability of the atmosphere of the cave or tomb where the cerements had lain, had never germinated. These grains, taken and deposited in the earth, came to life. Who knows, but the wheat stalk on which these grains grew, had decorated the coiffure of Cleopatra? And who knows that this wheat has not grown and exhibited a quality precisely such as it would have done, if planted in the ground the thirtieth summer before the coming of our Lord? Who knows? Certain it is, that the grain grew and wheat presumed to be like that of Cleopatra's times exactly, is now found on the shores of the Mediterranean.

If this can take place with the cereal plant, why might not the race of man in some places along those shores have remained intact? And why might not men like the old ones be now produced, give them the same opportunity?

Are there not valleys amongst those labyrinthine regions in which the race has never deteriorated? Nay, have not certain small societies of men shown at various periods since history flourished about the Mediterranean a heroism, a strength, a virtue, a talent, equal to that of the best of the ancient days? What of the Albigenses, the Waldenses? What of the Swiss? What of the Caucassians against whom the Czar of Russia brought all the powers he could apply to bear, and although he may have wearied them out he never conquered them.

Skim over the pages of the history of middle Europe during the last thousand years, and here and there will be found some village Fabius, who with dauntless breast the little tyrant of his fields withstood. Some mute inglorious Homer may still be found along these shores; some Cæsar guiltless of his country's blood. Let the rays of cotemporaneous history be concentrated upon that region, and what may be the effect. See now the Herzegovinians, living within a few score miles of Thermopylæ. Look at your illustrated journals, whose artists have given us portraits of their leaders. Does your English Lodge exhibit a finer set of features? Is not manly beauty, strength, character, intelligence, to be seen amongst these mountaineers? Why may not here be Cæsars, Hannibals, Pompeys, Antoniès, Demosthenes, Horaces, Virgils, Ciceros? Why? They are undeteriorated, as much so as the grain of wheat in the mummy. Is rural virtue constantly practiced for two thousand years to injure the human race? Surely not. And now they are aroused. What do they fight with? They have no money to pay for improved arms. They fight with spears, they resist the tyrant, and they may eventually conquer him.

From what has been said, it appears that this Mediterranean region, the seat of all history in former times, has had no history to speak of since the disruption of society at the final fall of the Roman empire. Men here have struggled toward prominence, nations have endeavored to rehabilitate themselves; but the spiritual party amongst them has always been in the ascendant, and kept them down. The dread of the Mysteries of Hereafter has been kept up before all these peoples, and those who have wielded its prospective terrors in the faces of men have always had their way.

Every species of government has been successively tried. Republic after republic sprung up in Italy. The keenest and brightest politicians have done all they could to arrange the social compact on a permanent basis. The Machiavellis, worldly but brilliant in intellect. The Guicciardinis, statists of the first rank, have given their minds to the problem; but the race has been drugged, as it were. It has slept, or has gone through life in a waking dream. The Church flourished. The teachings of the meek and lowly Jesus were framed into a worldly science, and the simplest and easiest duty that was ever laid before man to perform has been turned into a juggle. Bell, book and candle, incense, surplice, grand cathedrals, dim religious light, music, painting, poetry, have all been exhausted to mystify and magnify a system that had but two rules, which could be written on the palm of one's hand; for on "these two laws" hang not "all the law and the prophets?" He who runs might read. But this did not suit the close corporations having man's eternal interests in charge. The mysteries of the dark future, puzzling to all, inscrutable to all, were pretended to be understood by a body of men, one of whom held his commission directly from on High. This body has been managed with a worldly wisdom unsurpassed. Every weakness of mankind, every foible has been taken advantage of to sustain it. Its finger must be in all his affairs. The secrets of the bureau, the secrets of the boudoir, of the family, of the court, of the forum, were all known and taken advantage of.

Nay, the secrets of the inmost hearts of individuals were in possession of members of this body. Were not these noted, collected, arranged, analyzed, taken in singularity and plurality, individually and collectively, and from these were not policies to meet every possible contingency educed? Always in the interest of this immense close corporation. Had it not auxiliary societies attached—"side shows," as it were. Where things were to be done which were unseemly perhaps for the main body, could not the Society of Jesus take them up? Every human precaution which it was possible for the mind of man to imagine was taken in order to maintain this Church as a corporate body, and to keep its ascendency over mankind. What could possibly be the result of this? Human advancement? Not at all. Human retardation, or human arrestation. Advancement might endanger the Church.

Keep society where it is and the Church will retain its earthly power. Hence the Mediterranean is surrounded with cities of the dead. Hence colonization abroad resulted badly. The colonists were held by a thread which was fastened to the chair of St. Peter. No change in society is to take place although the colonists seek new fields in which to prosper. The cathedral, the monastery, the nunneries follow them. Nay, the Inquisition follows them. Could such colonies flourish? Let Peru, let Chili, let Cuba, let Mexico answer. The shores of the Spanish main became as torpid as those of the Mediterranean. The manners of the people to-day are like what they were long centuries ago. All colonies around these people have prospered, have gained autonomies for themselves. Nay, have taught their brethren of the old world that republicanism is possible. And that man can arrange his affairs with his God without a system of official attorneys. Men can read their bibles in their closets, can take the advice of the Mediator, and praying to Him in secret know that he will reward them openly. Where Independence has gone forth with the colonists there has been success, advancement, wealth, enterprise. Results have shown that creation meant progress and expansion, not "thus far shalt thou go and no further." And even at home, enfolded though society may have been with the wrappings of a mummy, some grains of wheat have crept into the folds. There are valleys and fastnesses amongst the Alps, the Appenines, the Caucassus, the Pyrenees, the Jura, the Tyrol, and elsewhere, where small portions of the race remain unchanged. These have borne persecution through many a long century. Sometimes when cut to the quick there would be recalcitration, but in general they have borne their cross—following Him as He told them. The cross has been heavy, but it has been ably borne. There has been no breaking down amongst some of these people. There are seeds that will give yet fruit like the ancient fruit, even as the Egyptian wheat fructifies in earth two or three thousand years older than that in which itself had grown.

Thus these abuses or misuses of the mysteries that always attend and continually perplex nations, have kept down the energies of the population of the world's ancient seat of empire. Nor Rome, nor Byzantium, nor Mecca, nor Medina, have utterly trodden out the garden bed. Weeds have grown there and well nigh choked it up. But beneath the noxious, useless vegetation there are roots and fibres biding their time. When the garden comes to be tilled over these will have a chance to spring up and the ground will no longer be cumbered.

Rome has not advanced. Though it has enjoyed power and used it unrelentingly. It is answerable for the Inquisition. It has perverted man individually and collectively. It has frightened the peasant and the prince, Jacques Bonhomme and Charles V., shaken the terrors of futurity before their eyes on their dying bed, and it has crazed equally the one and the other. It has turned millions of men into monomaniacs on the subject of religion.

It has been ever unrelenting. Knowing the results on society it instituted the monasteries, where the religious monomaniacs might spend their days protected from the shocks of the world. The monastery for the males, the nunneries for the females, whilst it kindly assumed the charge of the devotees' wealth.

And the Mussulman. What has he done; he and hishigh priests? He saw that something more sensuous was required for the truculent nature of those who believe in his dogmas; and he therefore admitted polygamy. But polygamy carried with it its own cure. License sexual indulgence, and enervation of the race must come sooner or later. True, the system has lasted a long time. It has lasted twelve hundred years, but enervation is at last approaching, and atrophy must result. .

The region under consideration has been under both these spiritual systems, and their time is fast approaching. The hardy northern islanders have spread their language over large portions of the globe. They have proclaimed man's universal brotherhood. All men are created equal. For this they have fought and bled; fought against the foreigners, fought amongst themselves.

Freedom of speech, of the press, of worship, universal education. They have utilized the steam engine, they have snatched the lightning from heaven, and the rod from the tyrants. These things are beginning to be known in the old seat of government of the world. They have made it possible for one people to govern themselves, though occupying half a hemisphere. If they can do this on what is called the new side of the world why cannot the same be done in the old? If the Mediterraneans of North America can be made free of access to all nations, why cannot the old Mediterraneans be the same? Are not the cases analogous? Are not the localities of the waters homologous in respect to the physical geography of the territory? These questions come home to men's business and bosoms. Why shall there be turnpike gates set up at every little strait connecting two branches of the same sea? Why shall the English hold Gibraltar and question every shallop that passes the Pillars of Hercules? Why shall the passage of the Red sea be in the hands of a single nation? Why shall the Sultan hold the straits of the Bosphorus and the Dardanelles, and say to the nations fronting on the Black Sea, you may pass here, but your passage shall be restricted. You must report to me. You shall have but so many vessels on the Black Sea. You shall have no more. Your Danubes, your Volgas, your Dons, and your Dniepers, can send their products forth, but in so many ships. I question the propriety of your penetrating further East. If you make railways or ship canals along the Caucasus to the Caspian it will be at your own risk. If you connect yourself with the Euphrates, you are infringing upon my territory.

But will the Czar stand this limitation any longer? The Yankee, he says, sends forth the riches of the Mississippi valley through the Gulf of Mexico to any porton the ocean. The great lakes and the St. Lawrence deliver their products where they please. Why am I to be restricted? The northern part of the western hemisphere may be crossed by a railway. Why may not a similar railway be constructed from the Black Sea to the Caspian? From the Caspian to the wealthy inlands or uplands of Asia? The world belongs to man, and man has certain inalienable rights on all parts of it.

I call out for the *Freedom of the Seas*. That is the Eastern question. The Atlantic is free, the Pacific is free. Why may not the Mediterranean be free? Measure its coasts, including the banks of the rivers, and those coasts run up to scores and scores of thousands of miles.

They represent every climate and every production of the earth, as much as the coasts of the great oceans do. This is the Eastern Question, and it must and shall be answered.

If there be a St. Lawrence, a Hudson, a Delaware, an Ohio, a Mississippi, and if these be free, why may not the Danube, the Volga, the Dan, the Dnieper, and the rest? Cannot man return to the old home farm, and cultivate it as of old? Because a mosque or a church is to be kept up may not commerce be free?

But now comes the difficulty. Open the Mediterranean and its accessories and what becomes of the East Indian monopoly? Make a ship canal from the Black Sea to the Caspian, and you get fully three thousand miles of direct eastern navigation. Let avenues extend beyond the Caspian, and the very heart of the East is penetrated. The great tributaries of the Mediterranean can be improved. Great valleys can be recultivated. The Euphrates will again teem with commerce. Mankind will find occupation. But can this be done without war? The Turk accustomed to his ways and his luxuries, his harems and his kiosks, in which to lazy away the long summer afternoons—enjoying a *dolce far niente* unquestioned for hundreds of years, lording it over virtuous, industrious races of pure and harmless Christians; sustained by taxes levied upon their industry. Is this to last forever? If this part of the earth was to stand accursed for a period has not the period nearly terminated? Are not the races who proved rebellious in the old time and would not understand or receive thankfully the good which the Almighty provided them—are they not sufficiently punished? Have not the sins of the fathers been visited on the children for a sufficient number of generations? Shall they not have another chance? They are beginning to arouse from their slumbers. They are beginning to bestir themselves. Individuals of them have visited other regions; have seen and enjoyed freedom, and have written home. This has been going on for a century. A hundred years since it was declared emphatically and afterward enforced, that all mankind were born equal. This declaration has taken root amongst the nations and yokes have since that time been thrown off. Why may not the original Caucassian race be free? Why may they not have independence? But why may not the oceans be free to all? What means this restriction? At every strait there is a fort; and these forts are sustained by foreign nations. It costs money to sustain these forts; and no nation will spend money without a return any more than a man will. The Mediterranean waters should be free to the world, let whoso may say ought to the contrary.

This question must be settled. Italy is interested—France, Spain, Austria, Egypt, Palestine, Persia, Morocco, Russia. Let those waters be covered by propellers. Let all the debouching waters have a chance to connect. Let there be no restrictions. Let the way be as open as the Straits of Magellan, or even as the British Channel. Let Russia make internal improvements having their termini on these waters. But let her works be free to all who will pay a fair freight. In a word, let there be no monopoly. But this would create a ruinous competition as against the trade of England with India. *Let it!* All the better. Did Britain consider the Venetians when she set up her transportation round the Cape? And now if there be an easy way by the interior; if there be an easier way, in God's name let it be opened. It will be open to England as to the rest. The most enterprising nations will get the advantage. Open the Mediterranean. Let there be freedom of egress and regress. But above all, let there be religious freedom. If the Turk will not enjoy his religion peaceably by the side of the Christian, drive him away. The Christian is learning very fast to enjoy his without interfering with others. But let the nations unite and *enforce peace.* Let them keep navies in these waters to command freedom. Let them join for their common interest. Let there be no monopoly of any pursuit which it is the inalienable right of all men to enjoy. Let there be, as has been said by somebody, a congeries of autonomial states, each guaranteeing justice to its subjects. Let these at last form a government like that of the United States of America, if possible. There is great difficulty in that plan at this time on account of the diversity of languages; but let there be free trade—let there be free intercourse, and that difficulty at last will cure itself. What a grand consummation is this for contemplation. Can it possibly be practicable?

If practicable on one hemisphere, why not on another? The imagination of a Cæsar never reached to such a height as this, and yet if men would only be quiet and consider the subject, it is entirely within the possibilities of the not very distant future. But such changes have never taken place; no great advancement has ever been made without the shedding of rivers of blood. Did not our Lord himself say when He was here, I bring you not peace but a sword! And He brought a sword indeed. The sod over which He passed; the soil on which His doctrines have been preached; ground over which He did not pass has been irrigated by blood. But the blood has not been spent in vain. Is this to be so forever? The national hymn of France declares that the impure blood of the invader shall fertilize the furrows of . her fields. The American national anthem cries out that the blood of the foe shall wash out the pollution of his footsteps. Is not the Freedom of the Seas also Freedom of Religion, and if it be, is it not a part of the mission of Christ as yet unperformed, and is it to be peace or a sword ?

· The cloud is rising on the eastern horizon no bigger now than a man's hand, but its edges are tinged with a lurid light; is it the reflection of blood? Alas! it is to be feared! But Freedom is coming. It must come. The garden spot of earth has been choked up with weeds for more than a thousand years. The garden spot must be weeded. The flowers of Freedom must have scope to grow—must have ample room and verge enough. Let us pray God that the consummation may be allowed to take place without a deluge of blood.

English statesmen are placed in an exceedingly embarrassing position by this state of things. It is plainly to the interest of England that the Mediterranean shall remain in its partial desuetude, for thus there is little or no competition against her monopoly of the East India trade. It is to her interest that the Turk shall be undisturbed, for while he holds his European empire the Mediterranean trade will not revive. It is England's interest to sustain and help him even. But he cannot live it seems without harrassing Christian communities. He cannot live without imposing unjust burthens upon them—burthens which they are constantly rebelling against—constantly endeavoring to throw off. And it is unseemly in the greatest of Christian nations to take part against the oppressed of her own belief. Yet not to take part encourages other nations to compete against England.

If the Dardanelles be made absolutely free the Czar comes in upon the shores of the Black Sea—his own territory, and establishes rival navies to that of England—with advantages of location far superior to those of England. Nay, the Czar may monopolize a power over the whole of those waters—a power that well may set itself up against all that England can do. The Czar may, in other words, assume an undue preponderance of the balance of power against which the great nations of Europe have set themselves for many years, allowing no single nation to attain such preponderance. The Czar calls the Turk a "sick man"—unfit longer to hold extended empire in Europe, and as the Turk is his neighbor he looks to take his place when he dies or leaves. At the last outbreak England and France, or rather England and Napoleon III., united against the Czar to keep him from ousting the Turk—and even then the people of England wondered why the Cross of St. George was found assisting the Crescent. So it must have been also with the good Christian people of France, and the eyes of both are more open now than they were then; and they will wonder if they again be called into the field fighting under the banner of Mahomet. Besides France has other things to do now in arranging her government on a permanent republican basis. It is questionable whether she would join any power to sustain the Turk.

Spain has a large front on these waters—Austria also—and the Southern heathen nations. They all look with interest at the subject now, and we may be sure that Bismarck has at least one eye quite open to this subject.

How to please all—to satisfy all—this is the Eastern Question. Like all great questions, it ought to be easy of arrangement, if it be settled on principles of "equal and exact justice" to all men. Let the waters be made free as those of the Atlantic—as those of the Pacific. Let all unite to do what is right for all. But when did man in such a dilemma ever do exactly the right thing? When was ever such a question arranged without bloodshed? Is man better now than he was ever known to be before. It is much to be feared that he is not, and again the world may be prepared to hear of the ensanguination of the midland waters. Again may he the multitudinous sea incarnadine. But may we not hope through all to see justice established in that region where for so many ages man has fought like the carniverous beast for supremacy. Fought without reason—fought without justice. Fought merely to attain and retain by force real or supposed advantages. Never ceasing to fight until overcome by sheer exhaustion he was compelled to say to his enemy as the quarrelsome child says, let me alone and I will let you alone.

May we not, however yet hope that peace may reign, and prosperity, the consequence of enlightened competition, result amongst the remains of the old nations. Amongst the "Ruins" that set the skeptical Frenchman of the last century to thinking. Have nineteen centuries of the teaching of the Mediator gone for nothing? Have we not rebelled against Him, argued against Him, questioned His authority, used Him as a talisman to gain riches by,? Have we not died for Him and killed for Him? And is He not all the purer or (being perfect from the beginning,) have we not at last found that He is perfect and perfection in all things? Have we not at last found Him to be all-sufficient? Surely we have. Let us then join and in *His* name at last place these waters at the service of all, as they were no doubt originally intended to be. As the great oceans were—as the atmosphere is. Let each nation surrounding them cultivate its soil and practice the industries for which it is by climate adapted; and let there be exchange and barter of commodities and increase of manufactures. Let there be brotherhood. There is room enough for all. Even here, within or surrounding our ellipse, there are wide regions left uncultivated.

The Asiatic nations have taught us that vastly greatly numbers of men can be sustained upon the earth's surface than have ever assembled in any part of Europe. There is room to quadruple any population in Europe and sustenance sufficient produced by the soil before there need be any serious crowding.

As to living and living in peace, have we not rules under which if we live we cannot fail? Has not the "Son of man" given us these "two laws," and are they not all-sufficient for our ethics? And though we may never reach their perfection, can we not keep on trying? And as to our politics, have we not tried in very large numbers and upon a very large surface the golden rule of justice to all of whatever clime or complexion? Have we not tried this now for a hundred years? (Witness the Centennial celebration in the United States)—and is it found wanting? Let us have universal education. Let us bring up our youth in the principles of the Son of God, and in the practice of justice to their fellows, and can we fail? Let us begin. The time has arrived. The Turk will either change his style of government or he must retire from Europe. If he will adopt our principles, and he says that his Koran teaches what our Testament teaches. Be it so. Then let him act under the teaching. We can live together. But if he must go, let him. The more southern climate may suit him better. If he goes then none but Christians will remain. Let these purify themselves. Let them return to the simplicity of the early fathers. Let there be no abracadabra in the worship of God. Let the motto be, Jesus Christ and Him Crucified, and all *must* be well. It cannot be otherwise. And the garden spot will smile again. Nay, will prove almost a Garden of Eden—made for the enjoyment of mankind in his latter days—a garden from the enjoyment of which he has been precluded by reason of his own perversity for so many ages. Let there be no bloodshed, if possible. But if it begin, let all Christendom unite to stop it, to staunch it, as soon possible. Thus may the great Eastern Question be settled for the permanent benefit of the human race.

Meanwhile England is pretty well fixed for eventualities. Her guns bay the moon from Gibraltar, and she has other stations on the Mediterranean. She has bought the Suez Canal, and we may be sure she will soon let the world see that she owns it.

She has a station at Aden on the Straits of Bab-el-Mandeb, so that the Red Sea is an English canal. Her navy scours the Indian Ocean, and she has fortifications upon the coasts of the Peninsula. She can afford to keep quiet and let events take their course. If the Turk gives up or loses Constantinople she will doubtless be in at the death, and will want to know how things shall be closed.

Yes England is well prepared for eventualities in a material way. But there is another question. How is the conscience of the Great British Christian people to be satisfied, when asked to gratify the sordid interests of trade in contravention of the Christian sentiment? The trade of the nation may be jeoparded by non-interference here, but are the interests of the nation's soul to be placed in peril by assisting the Crescent at the expense of the Cross? Will the people of England be induced again to draw the sword in favor of Mahomet for the sake of a few "rascal counters?" It is a question of casuistry, and it may well be predicted that come what may, the great English people will bear in mind the motto, God Defend the Right. Not only were they, but also were the French, fooled into a profane, unholy war twenty years ago. When the Crescent and the Cross appeared on the same side and in this very field. It is to be questioned whether France would have joined England then had her affairs not been guided by Napoleon III., not the wisest of her modern statesmen. That stupendous wrong will hardly be repeated—for the French at last are giving up their minds wholly to putting their house in order; and as to the English they will remember their sacrifices in 1856. They will remember the "six hundred," and they will reflect that do as they will it will only be a putting off of the evil day as it was before. The consequences will be momentous. The predominance of London as the metropolitan capital of the world may be lost. The predominance of Paris—in her way—and somewhere on the Mediterranean shores may again arise the world's capital. One of the great Œcumenical crises is impending— another mile post in the world's historical pathway is about being set. An era approaching. No nation can put it off. The commencement of the decay that will make Macaulay's, or rather Volney's, "solitary traveler at London bridge" possible, may be indicated by the present probable disturbance. The efforts to stop it, the exertions of the strength of the greatest nations will avail nothing. Such efforts will simply stain the cotemporary pages of the world's history with blood—to mark the era for future reference. Let men, let nations reflect. Let them retire to a place of safety, that they may not be overwhelmed by the cosmical change about to occur. These grand events are always right in their consequences. Let no puny whipster of a "statesman" try to avert them. There is indicated in cotemporaneous history a tendency toward universal human freedom—and let us hope toward human brotherhood also. The Eastern Question is one of the evidences of that tendency. Let us remember—THY KINGDOM COME, THY WILL BE DONE ON EARTH AS IT IS IN HEAVEN.

POSTSCRIPT—SOLUTION.

Let the nations bordering upon the Mediterranean agree amongst themselves to guarantee the freedom of its waters to the world, as the great oceans are now free; and there is not enough power in any or all adverse interests, real or supposed, to prevent the happy consummation which would result from such an agreement. Could this be done before the year 1900 it would add a brilliant burner to the candelabrum of great lights, which already make this century the most illustrious in the world's history.

CPSIA information can be obtained
at www.ICGtesting.com
Printed in the USA
BVHW041041170119
538075BV00017B/865/P

9 780259 496250